we are already ourselves

Mbumba J Banda

Presentation by *BookLeaf Publishing*

Web: www.bookleafpub.com

E-mail: info@bookleafpub.com

ISBN: 9789363300521

First edition 2024

To every soldier that fights with pen and upon paper. I stand on your shoulders.

Anthu anga: my God, my friends, and my family

I am, because you are.

ACKNOWLEDGEMENT

My friend, Qabaniso Malewezi

Thank you for carrying me this far.

PREFACE

Believe me,

Your incomprehensibility is worth writing about.

1. Earthling

You are layers of life and loss
sequences of living and wandering
the very thing of museums and poetry.

Spirits seek the opportunity to enthrall you
Many stare in awe at the brilliance of your
evolution.

How fearfully you've evolved has all the
caterpillars astounded.

We call you freedom;
for you are made of the same science that causes
earthquakes.

How dare you?!
see anything less than quintessential
when you look at you.

2. Rhyme

I bet your heart is actually a beatbox

and your soul a music player.

I bet you the heavens listen to you

on repeat.

3. Acquaintances

I know of pain,

of the weight of crushed hope
of the pressures of perfection
and of the curses flung from the lips of cruel
lovers.

I know too well the fear of rejection
the prickling possibility of abandonment
merged with the stings of failure.

And what of the storms of unwanted grief?
of bargaining with God
of hoping to steal more time
to offer yourself in exchange for a loved one

of the desire to marry the earth
in the hopes of escaping ghosts.

I know of the exhaustion of a soul
starved of love and affirmations.

I know of an empty stomach and a hardened
heart
of rock bottoms and cold graves.

It was there that I learned of resurrection
came face to face with the saving grace of
eternal love
became aware
of the healing balm of mercy
found in another broken,
trembling torso.

I have come to know forgiveness and laughter.
Come to understand the magic of catching a
smile in your own reflection

the power of falling into the laps of those you
call home

the grace of spaces that allow you to be bruised,

to be figuring it out,

to be not knowing,

not having all the answers,

to be not perfect

to be bitter,

broken,

biased,

to be human,

to be.

4. Haunting

There is a girl who looks like me
Her patience is much shorter than mine
her eyes spades of judgment.

She is about as tall as regret
with lips that recount my every failures
her love,
a lie.

She has made a habit of haunting the halls of my
future
attempting to convince everyone who will listen

that I am a broken thing

of a broken reputation

have loved broken people

and aren't worthy of trust.

Inside her throat lies buried my every sin

Every lie I ever told

Every heart I shattered

Every secret spilled before its time.

In her tales, I am very much the monster
The gouling goblin,
carnivorous,
cancer -
that kills everything she touches.

The truth is,
She is right.

When you come across that black shadow of my
past,
and she tells you of the time I laid with Lucifer
only after pouring water on that sun-skinned
black boy.

hear me
I was in need of a savior
& He came.

5. Stillness

Stand Tall.

Tie Laces Of Humility On Your Shoes

Push Back The Cap Of Frustration From Your Shoulders

Breathe.

You are man enough.

It's in your demeanor

It's in your stance

Tell Your Shoulders They Have Nothing To Prove.

Don't Apologize For The Love Your Mother Left In Your Tone When You Speak.

Tell Them,

You've Been Loved Well

And Your Mellow Voice Is Proof.

And If They Would Desire A More Outward
Expression Of Your Masculinity.

Tell Them,

It Is None Of Their Business.

Be Still.

You Have Nothing To Prove.

6. Tender

He's not always a force of confidence

doing exactly what he's doing and looking good
at it.

Sometimes he's a fragile heart.

unsure as to why he's doing what he's doing in
the first place.

He needs love

that sees beyond the roccstar gimmicks and
carves a place in herself

For both of them,

to love and retreat.

a love that allows him to come without the
expectation of having to keep it all together,

like they demand.

7. M

'tis the summer of '22
you're wearing your confidence like a king's kufi

my hair is red
& the air smells like tangerines

your arms resemble sanctuary,
here I fall.

anxiety leads to twirling of rings on thumb and
pinky finger.

stay.
I have built you an empire in my mind.

the masses are grooving to afro-gospel.
full of the Holy Spirit, no power.

that wiggle in my hips, mischievous smile;
- amapiano is playing.

you speak fire into my bones,
how you elongate that 'Mm' sound when you say
my name.

hang on,
we could be the start of something special.

12

8. city of lost angels

There's another version of the world

Where people feed off my fault lines

Make trophies out of my mistakes

And make me feel,

a lot less of a mess

in comparison

9. how to stop falling in love
with people that will never
love me back:

10. She

She is not me,
but we are the same.

She may be wearing a velvet sweater with white
sneakers.
She may have curly hair, tinted at the edges.
She may be sleeping with her lover to prove a
point.
She may be wearing a black hijab with a nose
ring.
She may sometimes wear colorful makeup, may
be the head of the sports program, frequently on
the dean's list.
She may be sitting right next to you.

Surely she's bold; you'd have no reason to
suspect
that she doesn't have it all together,
that she has the same marks on her skin and soul
that I do.

The abuse is what we have in common

11. strong woman

You ever think maybe it's okay to cradle into a
ball of warmth and cry.
Maybe let your soul sistas into your mess so you
aren't so lonely.
You think maybe you could give yourself a
break and maybe put off that strong woman
facade and rest.
like without expectation.
like in full vulnerability.
like a tired traveler taking time to mend her soul.

How else will you pour into them if you're
empty?

12. dear you,

I hope you find a love that sings to you
folds itself into meaningless jokes
and makes you laugh your anxiety away
may their voice sound like a hummingbird's
song on an early morning after a dark
tumultuous night
I hope this love is a loud one,
affirming you out loud, loving you publicly
pampering, passionate, patient
may they have hands like home
able to carry the cracks of you
as they rock you back and forth until the storms
of life subside
you will remember your worth
everytime that you catch your reflection in their
eyes
you will feel like a skyline
high, mighty, glorious
the way that they look at you
will be poetry for a poet
healing for your identity
a reminder that even after all you've done
somebody loves you
and perhaps this will be the first time that you
believe in the miraculous

this,
and every day after that

13. Child of God,

19

I Heard Your Bloodline Is Royalty.

14. Malawi

When you see mountains
peeping above clouds in search of water
know, that you are witnessing a narrative in full
swing.

Say you come across the waters
behaving like a canvas for spilled hues of
sunsets and sunrises
they bring them to you in warm hummings of
swishing waves
know, that you are witnessing a nation at its
peak

The stars turn the sky into a stage

The moon lights up the celestial runway

and before you have a moment to blink

The sun
dressed in morning
shy as light comes breaking in

No, there is nothing like the Malawian sunrise

When she rises,
we rise with her into a new era,
carrying with us a boatload of memories gifted
to us by our forefathers.

In this land,
the rivers are a gathering of elders
drum circling around the tranquility of the lake
the hills clap and dance with thunderstorms
before the rain begins to form

They call us
aMalawi -
the warm heart of the Afrika

our land is filled with a mixture of hope and
laughter
beautiful ballads of blue skies and the endless
toil of a hardworking people

We are a smiling people
connected by the dense love letters in our skin

The only libraries we frequented
were situated around a fire
aGogo had the best books down in her memory
and although we heard it a million times
the story about how the kalulu outsmarted njovu
We watched her,

heart pumping at her every word

She had a way of taking us into history,
we became time travelers
discovering things about our land that cannot be
translated into the English

aMama would yell "eheh, you shall find the
nsima finished"
And immediately we were sucked right back
into the present
where the love of Ababa sweetened the wounds
of discrimination & lack

we wear our scars,
we wear our scars like angoni carry their shields
keeping one foot forward ngati tikuvina lipenga

we make everything our own
added bubbles to the English we speak

No, there is nothing like the Malawian way of
life

The way that bus vendors maneuver around the
town,
you'd think,
death is only a myth to them

while the women are walking testaments of
power and persistence

where I'm from
hips were made to carry babies
and the women have those too in abundance

know, there is nothing like the Malawian way of
life

the stories in our bones and secrets we hold

We are more than HIV commercials
feed the children
& stop poverty projects

We,
We are the black crescent moon of our land
raised high above all nations

we are stars in perfect alignment,

the roaring rage of blood spilt over emancipation
a greenery of warm wishes
we are full

Malawi is dressed in the hopes and fears of her
people
she makes no apologies for being all that she is,

has been

but with a Tonga like confidence

She presses on
eyes fixed on the rising sun

15. some day,

25

I won't let my outward appearance define me.

16. no more,

giving of myself to spineless images of mortal
men
bitter to taste
never learnt that flavor stems from their
relationship with YAH

no more,
throwing water on my flame to accommodate
fearful men.
the music in me,
I won't tune down to make you more able to
dance to the vibrations built into my spring
rhythmed soul

no more,
accommodating purposeless men
I am not a shelter for lost souls.

17. how to start a house fire

keep the windows open
find the ugly can of gasoline your father kept in
the back of the garage
tremble at the memory
get a good pair of gloves
you'll need your hands
you'll need your heart

pour the gas over the wooden floor
let it seep into the basement
into the folds of every wretched memory
every time they called you less than
every time you let yourself go

chain the 30 pound monster under the bed to the
beams in your room
position him right next to the devils that haunted
you
look them in the eye
then pour gasoline all over those suckers

douse the rest of the house
the attic
the little space in your closet you keep the curse
words

the lies
the knives you found in your back
the kitchen
the bathroom
the mirror in the bathroom that made fun of your
stretch marks and the color of your face

reach for the lighter
pull the ignition button towards you with your
index finger

look the flame in the eye
smile

toss it to the ground
then dramatically walk away

get in your car and drive away
slowly
trembling as you watch
the bright red flames
consuming all

this time laugh
there is no going back

these ghosts have haunted you enough.

18. clan

my little brother is quick to apologize
He says love is bigger than any one argument.

my sister is always watching telenovelas.
she says she never wants to forget that love
exists,
even if exaggerated

my mother sometimes prays with her eyes open
she says she never wants to miss her miracle.

my father is always dreaming
he believes the world is made for dreamers.

my auntie is always playing her music on loud
she says she'll take any chance she's given to
celebrate life.

my uncle is always taking pictures
he says some things are worth remembering.

ms Angela is always giving
she says that's what hands are made for.

Isabel is always singing.
she believes that one song can save a life

19. Birdsong

teach me to not think highly of myself

teach me to not conjure up insecurities from the
lips of unknown faces

teach me to marvel at my reflection

teach me to catch glimpses of my beauty in the
eyes of the sun

teach me to love myself,
always

teach me to believe in me,
especially when my circumstances and my
clothes say otherwise

teach me to enjoy the simplicity of this life

teach me to stop crucifying myself on the
crosses of social media

teach me how to be me,
fearlessly

teach me to fly,
high above the need to people please

teach me to look to you for approval
and not dying men
shadows cast
fleeting things

teach me to listen to nature's stories of you

teach me to smile because you've given me a
good life and made promises of a better one

20. Afterthought

One day,

you will hear stories

of how

I made friends with gratitude

welcomed into my heart

self love

how I,

no longer get along with trauma

unforgiveness and I

no longer move in the same circles.

I will be somewhere

in between laughter and purpose

living on,

without fear.

21. New Day

You mustn't be bitter

with yesterday

nor fault the sun

for its lack of shine

you mustn't shut your heart

to light & love

nor chain up hope

in memories of heartache

You mustn't

replay your mistakes

nor torture yourself

with regret

None of us

are the same people we were

yesterday.

9 789363 300521